ATTITUDE

The Cornerstone of

LEADERSHIP

Pat Sullivan

This work is dedicated to my wife, Peg, my children, Colleen, Katie, Pat, Anne, and Bridget and all the young men I was privileged to coach.

TABLE OF CONTENTS

CHAPTERS

Introduction to Pat Sullivan

By Tom Kennedy

In my role as a business marketing director, I have seen dozens of motivational speakers and leadership authorities present at a wide array of conferences and company events. Like other business managers, I have read dozens of leadership books, many containing highly credible research and interesting statistics. Most of these books and speakers have informed and inspired me at least in some small way.

No one person, however, has had a more profound and lasting impact on me and my views of leadership than Pat Sullivan. Pat was both a teacher and coach to me during my undergraduate college years. Because of his relentlessly positive attitude and uncompromising high regard for his fellow human beings, I believe there is no greater authority on the subject of leadership.

It is altogether fitting that Pat write this book on the key characteristics of leadership, because he exemplifies all of the qualities discussed herein. Ironically, all of the people he has chosen to highlight here for their leadership skills would just as easily point to Pat himself as a terrific role model.

Leadership, as featured in MBA schools, centers on the study of personal traits and behaviors: from organizational skills, vision, and integrity to communicating and modeling the way. All of these elements are important, but without a positive attitude and a healthy respect for others, the discussion is more academic than practical. Both of these attributes are core to the character of Pat Sullivan.

Had he selected sales as his profession instead of teaching and coaching, I have no doubt that his list of credentials and lifetime achievements would be just as long as it is now. He has the remarkable ability to make every person he meets feel like the most important person in the world. But despite his excellent social skills, he's not the least bit interested in selling anything. People, teaching, and continuous learning are what he cares most about.

He has portrayed a positive attitude in every possible life situation. In the sports arena, it didn't matter if his team won by twenty points or lost by the same margin, Pat would always tell the team what it needed to hear: all of the good, the bad, and the ugly. Indeed, his communication skills are on the same plane as his strategic and visionary skills. He could always find points of encouragement after difficult losses, even if such observations might have been lost on the other 99 percent of the people in the building.

The sum of his impact on his former students might best be illustrated by a practice I started early in my business career. Each time I had to prepare for a presentation or public speaking opportunity, I would create notes with the word *Sully* written inconspicuously outside the margins. This served as a visual reminder for me not only to be well prepared for my subject matter, but also to represent myself in the most sincere, caring, and positive way I possibly could. "Care about other people and they might care about my message," I would tell myself.

In this book, as in his public speaking appearances, Pat provides real-life examples and practical advice on how to improve leadership skills. The highly accomplished people documented here are clear testaments to the leadership traits Pat brings to life through the ATTITUDE acronym. By the same token, Pat Sullivan deserves to be recognized for his ability to inspire the leaders in all of us.

Tom Kennedy
Director of Marketing and Communications
Republic Financial Corporation
Denver, Colorado

Introduction for Coach Pat Sullivan

By Randy Stelter

When I reflect on Coach Pat Sullivan, one word continually comes to mind: *magnanimous*. I first met Coach Sullivan forty-six years ago. I was an impressionable ten-year-old, and my best friend's father coached at Providence Catholic High School in New Lenox, Illinois, with Pat. I recall sitting at my friend's kitchen table after games and listening with rapt attention to Coach's stories. Hours later my sides were hurting from laughing. Coach Sullivan had this gift of always making others laugh. His stories were hilarious and yet inspiring.

As the years went on, I begged my father to allow me to attend Providence to play for Coach Sullivan, but Dad told me we were not Catholic and we could not afford the tuition. However, fate always has a way. When Coach Sullivan became the head basketball coach at the University of St. Francis in 1976, I received a call from him. My dream came true, and what an honor it was to be able to play for and then coach with this great man.

If there is any one person who should be considered an expert on attitude, it is "Sully." I witnessed his leadership, his passion, his poise, and his professionalism daily. There is no doubt that Coach Sullivan left a legacy. For those of us who know Sully, his enthusiasm and his joy for life is infectious. His values, his magnetic personality, and his uncanny ability to get the best out of those with whom he works with and mentors make him the best to convey the concepts of attitude as described in this book.

Not only was he our coach, but he was the best college professor I ever had. Whether on the court or in the classroom, his mental toughness never ceased to amaze me. It was not only his work ethic but, most importantly, his integrity that was the foundation on which we based our trust and respect. Those of us who were fortunate enough to play for him wanted to emulate these attributes in our own lives.

Coach Sullivan could have coached at any Division I university. He is that good. However, his loyalty to USF President Dr. Jack Orr and Sully's own mentor and head baseball coach Gordie Gillespie was so fierce that no one could sway his passion for and commitment to the University of St. Francis. It is because of his values, his leadership, and his loyalty that the recreation center at the University of St. Francis was named in honor of him.

Coach Sullivan's concepts have been the "Cornerstone" that has guided me in my thirty-four years as an educator, coach, and athletic administrator. I am eternally grateful for his mentoring and his friendship. It is my belief that after you read his book, you will be as passionate about life, leadership, and attitude as he is and has made me.

Randy Stelter
Director of Athletics
Wheeler High School
Valparaiso, Indiana

About The Author

Pat Sullivan was a successful basketball coach, teacher, and administrator in the Chicago area for forty-four years. His high school and college teams won 599 games in his career, and he was named Coach of the Year at the conference and state levels on twelve occasions and Coach of the Tournament in the prestigious National Catholic Basketball Tournament in 1986. He was named Coach of the Year in each of the four decades he coached. He has spoken at coaches clinics throughout America for the USA Coaching Clinics and has presented clinics and/or camps in Belgium, Austria, Ireland, and Greece. He has also spoken to businesses from Boston to San Francisco on leadership.

Among his many honors are valedictorian of his Lewis College graduating class, NAIA State of Illinois and the Great Lakes Region Athletic Administrator of the Year, and Community Leaders of America. Lewis University gave him the Distinguished Alumni Award in Education, and the Will County Chamber of Commerce presented him with their Lifetime Achievement Award. His career was recognized with two recent honors. He received the Illinois Basketball Coaches Association Buzzy O'Connor Award for lifetime contributions to Illinois basketball and had the recreation center at the University of St. Francis named the Pat Sullivan Center.

Coach has been inducted into the Chicago-land Collegiate Athletic Conference Hall of Fame, the Joliet/Will County Hall of Pride, and the Halls of Fame at Lewis University, the University of St. Francis, Providence Catholic High School, and the Illinois Basketball Coaches Association.

He is married to Peg Sullivan and has five children, Colleen, Katie, Pat, Anne, and Bridget, and eleven grandchildren.

THREE LEADERS

I had the great pleasure of working with three outstanding leaders whom I reference in this book.

Please allow me to introduce these three extraordinary men.

<u>Gordie Gillespie.</u> My college coach at Lewis College, later Lewis University, in Romeoville, Illinois, was Gordie Gillespie. I not only had the pleasure of playing basketball and baseball for Gord, but also worked with him for twenty-five years at the college—now the University—of St. Francis in Joliet, Illinois. We may never see another coach like Gordie, in terms of both his being a three-sport coach and of the remarkable success his teams had in all three sports. As a football coach at Joliet Catholic High School and the College of St. Francis, a basketball coach at Lewis College, and a baseball coach at Lewis, St. Francis, and Ripon College in Ripon, Wisconsin, his teams won an incredible 2,402 games. I cannot imagine any future coach ever accumulating this many victories. With 1,852 baseball wins, he is the winningest coach in the history of four-year college baseball, a sport he coached for fifty-nine years. Among his many honors, he is the only man in the Illinois Coaches Association Halls of Fame in football, basketball, and baseball. He has been inducted into seventeen Halls of Fame during his illustrious career. All of these accolades pale when compared to the impact he has had as a leader on the 2,500-plus student-athletes he has coached.

Bishop Roger Kaffer. I worked with a remarkable principal at Providence High School, now Providence Catholic High School, for six years. Father Roger Kaffer, later Bishop Roger Kaffer, came to Providence at a very tenuous time. In 1969 we had ten high schools in the Joliet Diocese, and due to the difficult financial times, Bishop Romeo Blanchette had formed a committee to study the finances at each school. The committee recommended the closure of Providence. The bishop subsequently vetoed his own committee's decision and named Father Kaffer as our principal in 1970. Among my duties at Providence, I served as an assistant principal and saw first-hand how he saved our school.

Father was a brilliant man, holding master's degrees in arts and education, licentiates in theology and canon law, and a doctorate in ministry. But his brilliance was a far second from his care, concern, and support for people. He was the best priest I have ever known.

Dr. John C. Orr. The third great leader I was fortunate to work with was Dr. John C. Orr, president of the College of St. Francis. St. Francis was in very serious financial trouble when Jack arrived in 1974. Not only was he fighting financial concerns, but there were only 436 full-time students upon his arrival. When he retired in 1997, St Francis had 4,200 students, including 3,400 part-time students on-campus and in nineteen states, and was in excellent financial shape. Like Father Kaffer at Providence High School, Jack saved a college financially and led it to national prominence. However, his leadership went far beyond finances and enhanced enrollment. As you will read in the following pages, it was his interaction and his dedication to our students that defined his presidency.

I have been very blessed to have these three fine men as leaders in my life. They definitely personified the characteristics of leadership in the ATTITUDE acronym addressed in this book.

THE GOSPEL and I DON'T KNOW

Leadership is all about ATTITUDE.

The daily attitude of a leader makes all the difference in the performance of any organization.

Having been a basketball coach for ten years at the high school level and thirty-four at the collegiate level, along with serving as the athletic director, athletic chair, and assistant-to-the-president, I have spent a great deal of time studying the important role that attitude plays in leadership. In this book I will use the word *attitude* as an acronym, giving each letter of the word a characteristic that exemplifies a good attitude in a leader. Most of my examples will come from my world—the world of athletics and education. I ask you to translate these characteristics to your particular role of leadership. And I hope you will find that these characteristics transcend athletic leadership and can be applied to leadership in any organization.

I believe any presentation, oral or written, has merit if it makes you think. I hope you will think about these characteristics of a leader's attitude and consider integrating them into your leadership position.

Before I get to the attitude acronym, I would like to share two concepts that encompass all the traits of leadership that will be addressed in this book.

The first concept comes from St. Francis of Assisi. (If you are not of the Christian faith, substitute your faith-based word for the word *gospel* in the following.) He wrote, "Preach the gospel; if necessary, use words." Certainly the words of a leader are important, but of far more importance is his or her daily example. I have been fortunate to work with some great leaders, and there is no question that the values these leaders exhibited daily far outweighed their words. They lived the characteristics of a great leader, and their example spoke much more loudly than their words.

I was in my first year as a head high school basketball coach, a young, naive twenty-six-year-old. Our Chicago area conference mandated that all head coaches attend the fall meeting of the Chicago Officials Association. This was my first experience observing a man who did not need words when he got up to speak.

There were at least one hundred referees in the room, and the entire conversation was about what bums, we, the coaches, were. The referees were all agreeing that the coaches were yelling at them way too much, and that the only way to deal with the coaches was to give them technical fouls. Every referee who spoke reiterated this sentiment, and the conversation was very animated. Then an African American official with gray in his hair stood to speak.

I had no idea who he was, but I knew he was "somebody" when the entire room immediately became silent—before he spoke! It was obvious he had the respect of everyone in the room. He did use words, but what happened in that room before he spoke was truly incredible. His words were few but they changed the entire tenor of the conversation. He said to his fellow referees, "I disagree with you fellows. When a coach gets out of line, I walk over to him and tell him I have a technical for you in my pocket. Don't make me use it." I found out later he was the highly respected Art White, the Big Ten's first black basketball official. That incident taught me at an early age that if you earn the respect of your co-workers by the values you live by, you don't need a whole lot of words.

The second overall concept comes from the seventy-fifth anniversary edition of *Fortune* magazine. The entire issue was dedicated to one of the most important things that a leader does— decision-making. They interviewed leaders from the business, education, political, and military fields on their theories of decision-making. In my opinion, the most insightful comment came from Jim Collins, the author of *From Good to Great*. He stated that the best decisions made in American business board rooms over the past twenty-five years, regardless of what the business might be, all began with the same three words from the leaders: "I don't know."

I have worked with leaders who believed they "knew" but no one else "knew." They were convinced they were experts, and they rarely listened to their constituents. These leaders were impossible to work with. I have also worked with leaders who were not afraid to say, "I don't know." Not only did they listen to their co-workers, they actively sought out their opinions. I felt these men and women were the strongest and most secure leaders that I worked with, and I truly enjoyed my time with them.

We had to beat a certain team to get to the NAIA National Basketball Tournament in 1994. They had the best offense I had ever coached against in college basketball. As we were preparing to play them, one of our assistants came to me suggesting a very different way to defend them. Initially, I thought it was the worst suggestion I received from my staff during the entire year. I "knew" how to guard their offense. I was the boss and I "knew." That night I got to thinking more about his idea and finally came to the conclusion that maybe he was right and I was wrong. We did put it in the game plan, and to this day I believe it was the single most important reason we advanced to the nationals. Jim Collin's three words were certainly true in this case: I didn't know.

"Preach the gospel; if necessary, use words." The values that a leader lives by define him more than his words. The daily example he sets and the way he treats people are how he preaches the gospel. Leaders not afraid to say "I don't know" are the strongest leaders and the leaders that people enjoy working with. They do know one thing for sure. They don't have all the answers. So they pick the brains of their team because they don't want to find answers; they want to find the best answers. They also realize you never know where the best answers will come from.

ATTITUDE

One person's attitude does make a difference and your philosophy of criticism is important to your communication skills.

The A stands for the word *attitude* and the very first concept I'd like you to consider is this: does one person's attitude truly make a difference? I think with all the negativism and cynicism that abound in our country today, many people would say no, my individual attitude really doesn't make a difference. If you believe that, the following are some examples to think about.

You probably agree that Adolf Hitler's attitude made a difference. The attitude that he was able to permeate through Nazi Germany certainly made a difference for approximately six million people of the Jewish faith. In 2010, I worked a basketball camp in Austria. Because I had read so much about the Holocaust, I asked the coaches if we were near a concentration camp and, if so, could they take me there. We were and they did. It is impossible to put into words my feelings as we went from room to room. Suffice it to say that an expression the poet William Wordsworth coined, "What man has made of man," said it all. You could not believe that man could do the horrific things that he did in that camp to his fellow man.

A good friend of mine encouraged me to read *Helter Skelter*, a book by Vincent Bugliosi, the prosecuting attorney in the Charles Manson trial. When I finished the book, I could not believe that anyone could inculcate the attitude that Manson inculcated in his "family" to commit some of the most heinous crimes in the history of our country. But he did.

On the other side of the coin, when Great Britain Prime Minister Winston Churchill was asked to speak at his alma mater, Harrow School, twenty-seven words from his speech may have epitomized the attitude of England during World War II more than all the volumes that were written on the war. He told the students, "Never give in. Never give in....Never give in except to convictions of honour and good sense....Never yield to the apparently overwhelming might of the enemy." He spoke these words on October 29, 1941, and there is no question that his leadership and his individual attitude made a difference for England during the war years.

Now I'd like to take you to Busch Stadium in St Louis. It is the fourth game of the 1967 World Series between the Cardinals and the Red Sox. I grew up with and played college baseball with a utility infielder on the Cardinals, Ed Spiezio, who went on to have great years with the Padres and White Sox. Ed got tickets for me and my dad to see the game.

Carl Yastrzemski was Boston's third hitter in the first inning, and Bob Gibson was on the mound for the Cardinals. If my recollection is correct, the first two pitches were thrown at Yastrzemski's knees and almost hit him. You knew something was going on, and sure enough, Gibson hit him on the next pitch. That incident made me think of another player that opposing pitchers regularly threw at, with two differences. They threw at his head, not his legs, and he wore no batting helmet because there were no helmets in his day. He also played arguably the worst position he could have played: second base. When opponents tried to steal second, they did not slide into the base. Instead, they came with their spikes high, trying to spike him in the face. To further exacerbate his dilemma, he signed a contract saying he would not fight for three years. So opposing pitchers could throw at his head and base runners could attempt to spike him, and he could not fight. But he was a fighter. He was a great running back at UCLA and on his death bed, while fighting heart disease and diabetes, Jackie Robinson was fighting for all the civil rights concepts he believed in. I believe the attitude of Jackie Robinson made a big difference for the black athletes in the Negro League, giving them the opportunity to advance to the Big Leagues.

One of the great difference makers of our time was Mother Teresa. Her attitude certainly made a difference for the poor, the lepers, and the dying of Calcutta. She developed sixty centers in Calcutta that ultimately led to two hundred worldwide centers. Through her leadership, she founded the Missionaries of Charity order that numbered over one thousand nuns by 1970. Her example taught the world the meaning of service.

When Rosa Parks refused to move from her seat on a Montgomery, Alabama, bus on December 1, 1955, her attitude made a difference. Her courage was the catalyst for a movement that changed the history of our country. Rosa Park's attitude definitely made a difference for the civil rights movement in America.

As mentioned earlier, I served as the head basketball coach and assistant principal to Father Roger Kaffer at Providence High School in New Lenox, Illinois, in the early 1970s. There I saw firsthand how one person's attitude does make a difference. We were fortunate to win the Chicago Private League championship in a great game. We played in a gym with a tile floor and seating on only one side of the floor. For this championship game, we had the stands filled; people were standing four deep around the periphery of the gym; and an estimated four hundred people were in the cafeteria, listening to the radio broadcast of the game.

That night Father Kaffer decided we needed a new gym. In the summer we developed a position paper delineating the reasons we needed it. We thought we had a great rationale for this addition. In the fall we assembled sixteen of the most influential people in our community at the home of Father Kaffer's parents. Father cooked the dinner, we passed out our report, and the discussion began. We expected full cooperation from this original committee. After two hours of discussion, Father called for a vote on whether we should initiate the plan. The vote was 16–0 that we should *not* proceed, due to the poor economic times. The committee felt there was absolutely no way we could raise the money in that economic environment.

There is only one reason Providence has a gym today: Father Roger Kaffer. Against all odds, he showed how one person's attitude definitely makes a difference. He got the tradesmen in our area to volunteer their time to help build the gym; he got parents, coaches, and faculty to volunteer their time; and he worked side-by-side with all the volunteers. He worked so hard, he broke his finger one day while running a backhoe. In addition to doing all this physical labor, he was almost singlehandedly responsible for all the fundraising to finance the building.

Therefore, I do believe that the attitude of one person does make a difference, and the attitude of the leader especially makes a difference. But the critical point is that the leader's attitude can have a positive or a negative influence on the organization. Some leaders build up an organization and some tear it down.

If a leader's attitude does make a difference, how he communicates with his people is very important. Especially important is how he criticizes those he leads. As a coach, I have to criticize the play of those who play for me, and as a leader, I have to critique the work of those who report to me. How do I criticize players and still have them keep their confidence, and how do I criticize employees and have them continue to come to work with a positive attitude? Because these concepts are vital to the success of a team or a business, I think it is important that a coach or a leader in any organization develop a philosophy of criticism. I certainly do not think the St. Francis coaching staff had the only - or necessarily the right - philosophy of criticism, but we did come to the following conclusions.

When. When would we criticize a player? If a player was physically lazy, we felt that had to be addressed. For example, if a player was lazy getting back to the defensive end of the court (everyone wants to run to the offensive end, because they might get a shot), he was not being fair to his teammates, and that was not acceptable. In a business environment, being late to work or to meetings or constantly delinquent in turning in reports is analogous to physical laziness on the basketball court. The second scenario in which we felt we had to criticize players was when they were mentally lazy. Once we taught a concept and we knew the player understood it, if that player failed to execute it, he was again being unfair to his teammates. This had to be addressed. My late father-in-law, Norman Fischer, the former CEO of Medalist Industries, called mentally lazy people "brain lazy." So our criticisms were founded in either physical or mental laziness.

What. Our next decision was what to criticize. In the great allegory *The One Minute Manager*, authors Ken Blanchard and Spencer Johnson stress that leaders should criticize the action, not the person. However, many leaders in my profession do not believe this. A number of coaches believe that you critique both the action and the person. They believe the only way you can win in athletics is to make players mentally tough. They believe athletics are like military boot camps, where the leaders break the soldiers down to build them up later. There is no question that athletic competition is tough and that coaches must develop mental toughness in their players to be successful. But players can take only so much personal criticism before they tune out the coach. On some teams I knew, the seniors would actually tell the freshmen that they had to tune out the coach when he was attacking their personhood, but tune him in when he was teaching basketball.

I played for a coach who believed in criticizing both the action and the person. I found it true that to keep my proper attitude and my confidence, I definitely had to tune him out when he was ripping me as a person. But I also found that when he began teaching basketball, I often still had him tuned out. Therefore, critiquing the action, not the person, made sense to me from both a personal and a teaching viewpoint.

How. How to criticize was our next decision. From everything I've read, one of the toughest coaches in American football history was the man for whom the Super Bowl trophy is named, the Green Bay Packers' legendary coach, Vince Lombardi. In his book *Instant Replay*, author Jerry Kramer, an offensive lineman on some great Lombardi Green Bay teams, added another element for leaders to consider when critiquing their team. He wrote that Lombardi could really be tough on you in practice, but when the practice was over, he often would put his arm around your shoulders and tell you, "Someday you will be the best lineman in the entire NFL." He added praise to the critique to uphold the player's confidence.

Morgan Wootten, the eminently successful high school basketball coach at DeMatha Catholic High School in Hyattsville, Maryland, was the first person I heard address the "sandwich theory." This theory states that we praise, critique, and then praise again, thus sandwiching the critique with praise. The praising affirms the person we are addressing, but we still have the opportunity to voice our criticism. I may tell our point guard, "You know you are a fine player, but why would you throw the difficult pass instead of the easier pass to keep our offense moving? Now get back out there and show everyone how an All-Conference player performs!" I affirmed his ability and achievements, but let him know the difficult pass was not acceptable. However, being of Irish descent, my temper did sometimes get the best of me, and I'd forget the praise.

I have two personal examples of criticism that I still remember from years ago. One was negative, the other positive.

I had just made the All-Star team in a high school Christmas holiday basketball tournament. We were at practice after the tournament and working on our press offense. Now, I very well may have been the worst dribbler in the history of the game. One dribble and I was done. So, needless to say, my dribbling skills were destroying our press offense. Then I heard the coach say sarcastically, "That's it. Just throw the ball to the *All-Star*." The emphasis was on the "All-Star." This was nothing different from what we heard daily, and it was very difficult to maintain a positive attitude in this environment.

Two years later, I was playing baseball at Lewis College. We had an outstanding team, one of the best in NAIA baseball; we finished third in the country in the 1963 national tournament. We were playing in the Chicagoland Collegiate Athletic Conference tournament and were the favorite team in the tourney. (We did win it most years.) I was a sophomore pitcher, and I entered the game in the seventh inning with the score tied. It was still tied in the bottom of the ninth, and we had our three, four, five hitters—great hitters—coming to bat in the top of the tenth inning. I had retired eight batters in a row, only to have the next three hitters get consecutive hits to give our opponents the win. Before I could leave the mound—feeling awful because I had let our team down—Gordie Gillespie, our coach, met me in the infield and told me, "Walk off this field with your head up. You will win more games for Lewis than you will ever lose."

Two critiques: I remember them both to this day. I was obviously more influenced by the latter critique. I am sure that is why when we lost a basketball tournament game in New York to the third-ranked NCAA Division II team in America, I had to address our best shooter. We lost the game on an opponent's shot right at the buzzer, and our best shooter took ten shots in the game and missed them all. If he had anything close to his normal shooting night, we'd win. We had to play again the next night, so I told him after our loss that if he was open in the next game and he did not shoot, I would take him out of the game. I assured him that he was going to shoot us to the national tournament at the year's end. He did just that.

Our philosophy of criticism led us to address— often harshly—physical and mentally lazy actions, not the person. We also often couched the criticism with praise.

Gordie Gillespie added another element in his philosophy of criticism: humor. One of his classic uses of humor was at a college football practice at St. Francis. Our team practiced next to a cemetery; a fence separated our practice field from a graveyard. One day our offensive unit was practicing timing plays with no defense. After the team ran the same play wrongly, not once, but three consecutive times, Gord went over to the fence. Leaning on it, facing the graves with his back to the team, he yelled to the graves, "Hey, fellas....Hey fellas....Make room for Gordie. These guys are killing me!" I think the kids got the message.

I hope these examples lead you to think about your own philosophy of criticism, because how we talk to our people, especially when we have to correct them, is both a critical and a sensitive element of leadership.

One person's attitude, and especially the attitude of the leader, does make a difference. The leader's attitude can enhance or impede the progress of his or her organization. How a leader communicates with his or her people, primarily in criticizing their performance, may be the most important factor in the morale of the organization. Leaders should strongly consider giving time to evaluating their philosophy of criticism.

Consider:

Give some thought to your attitude. Are your decisions making your organization better? And, how do you communicate with your people, especially when you have to critique their work? Are you hurting or enhancing their confidence?

TEAMWORK

Strong leaders build strong teams and give credit to their teams.

"Individual commitment to a group cause is what makes a team, a business, a church, or a country work." Vince Lombardi, Green Bay Packers.

"The main ingredient of a star is the rest of the team." John Wooden, UCLA

"It's amazing how much we can get accomplished when nobody cares who gets the credit." John Wooden, UCLA

"Either we all go uptown together or no one goes uptown at all." Al McGuire, Marquette

Each of the above three coaches is speaking to the most essential ingredient in sport: teamwork.

In the sport that I coached, basketball, the greatest shooter I ever saw play was Jerry West. He played fourteen years in the NBA and played on one championship team. Possibly the best all-around player I saw play, next to Michael Jordan, was Oscar Robertson. He actually averaged a triple-double one year, which is truly remarkable. He also played fourteen years in the NBA and played on one championship team. But Bill Russell played with the Boston Celtics for thirteen years and his teams won the NBA championship in eleven of the thirteen years he played. We were very excited in Chicago with the six championships captured during the Jordan era, so it is hard to imagine eleven championships.

I do not think you can win in athletics or in business without talent. You have to have talent to win, but the corollary to that statement is that talent alone will not win. Only talent that is willing to play together will be successful. The Celtics knew they had talent and that their talent was committed to teamwork, so during Russell's thirteen years, they made only two trades.

In the 1980s, two players changed the entire image of the NBA. During this decade, one or both of their teams played for the NBA championship nine times. Both these players, Magic Johnson and Larry Bird, were consummate team players. They truly made the players around them better with their unselfish team play. The same can be said for Michael Jordan. I had tickets for all the playoff games during the Jordan era. So, I did see the best-ever player at the most trying of times—the playoffs—and my conclusion was that Jordan, like Magic and Bird, was a great team player. He is the leading assist man in the Bulls history and, in this coach's opinion, he was not just the best defensive player on the Bulls. He was the best defensive player in the entire NBA! In addition to his passing and defense (we all know he was a prolific scorer), he was the mental leader of the team, and he led by example with his outstanding work ethic at practices.

The essence of athletics is definitely teamwork, but I believe teamwork transcends athletics. In his book *The Seven Habits of Highly Effective People*, Stephen Covey writes that when he consults with businesses, he finds three types of people: independent, dependent, and interdependent. The businesses that excel,

Covey writes, are those that develop interdependent people. They develop people who understand that excellence is reached only when everyone in the organization pulls together.

Father Roger Kaffer, principal at Providence High School, had two signs on his desk that described his management style. One we all have seen: "We can disagree without being disagreeable." The second I had never seen until I saw it on his desk: "None of us is smarter than all of us." And that is precisely how he led our school. He made the final decisions, but prior to making them, he actively sought the opinions of his staff and intently listened to their ideas. His management style was distinctly teamwork oriented.

In his book *Rising Sun*, Michael Crichton states there is quite a difference between the ways American and Japanese businesses initially look at a problem. In America, we tend to ask who is to blame for the problem, who caused the problem, and whose head has to roll. In Japan, their first impulse is to ask, how do we solve the problem? There is a vast difference between these two paradigms. The American way can destroy teamwork, whereas the Japanese philosophy can enhance it. All leaders can choose which of the two ways they want to deal with problems, because two things are for sure: there will be problems, and leaders must be problem-solvers.

I thought it was very interesting when a friend sent me a note from the Creative Educational Foundation that listed the skills desired by Fortune 500 companies when they were looking to hire personnel. The criteria were listed in their order of importance. Among the thirteen skills were problem-solving, creative thinking, and listening. But the number-one skill desired was teamwork.

The need for this particular skill definitely proved to be true with my children. When my daughter Colleen went to Sidley Austin LLP in Chicago and my daughter Katie to Arthur Anderson LLP, everything they did involved teams. The same was true for my daughter Anne when she joined Deloitte & Touche LLP and for my son, Pat, with IBM. My daughter Bridget, a former college lecturer and current competitive runner, credits her team of runners for helping her to develop into an elite marathoner. The lesson of teamwork learned from my children's athletic experiences carried right over to their business careers.

My mother and father certainly had teamwork in raising me and my brother and sister. We didn't have much financially, but we wanted for nothing. If we were poor, we sure didn't know it. As a nine-year-old, I definitely did not help our family finances. I had bothered my mom for weeks to buy a baseball. She finally relented and gave me two dollars to get one. I walked to town, bought the ball, returned home, and had batting practice with a friend. We managed to break a window that cost five dollars. That was a tough walk home, trying to figure out how I was going to tell mom about that window.

Though dad had a sixth-grade education, and mom went only through her sophomore year in high school, they were totally committed to our education. My siblings and I went to Catholic grammar school and high school, and it was just expected that we would go to college. All three of us became college graduates and spent our careers in education. Despite financial hardships, our parents' commitment to our education never wavered.

I don't remember mom or dad ever telling me they loved me. But they didn't have to tell me, because they showed it every day in every way. Today I tell my children after every conversation that I love them. I surely think that is important, but far more important is that, like my parents, I show it in all my interactions with them. Mom and dad exemplified their teamwork financially, educationally, and most importantly with their unconditional love.

As a twenty-five-year-old teacher and coach at Providence High School, I saw the importance of teamwork. In 1969 the school had less than five hundred students, and Bishop Romeo Blanchette's committee voted to close it. Parents, students, teachers, and administrators all worked together to petition the bishop to veto the decision. It was an entire community working as one that convinced the bishop to do so. Today Providence Catholic is a thriving high school in the Chicago Catholic League with an enrollment over 1,100 students.

The teamwork to keep Providence open was so unselfish that I do not remember one teacher ever talking about losing his or her job. The fight was never personal; it was to work as a team with students and parents to keep open a school we all believed in. It was a great learning experience for me as a young educator to see what can be accomplished when motivated people work as a team.

Finally, teamwork is not always, as Al McGuire used to say, "seashells and balloons." It is not all roses. Often there is adversity on teams, but if that adversity can be handled properly, it can bring a team closer together. I always appreciated the concept of "deposits in the bank" that Stephen Covey examines in his book, *The Seven Habits of Highly Effective People.* Covey's theory says that we all have "emotional bank accounts" with friends, teammates, family, and co–workers. These accounts start with a neutral balance, and just as with any bank account, we can make deposits and withdrawals. However, instead of dealing with units of monetary value, we deal with emotional units founded on trust. In other words, if we build trust with someone over time, we are afforded mistakes that won't destroy the relationship as a whole. If we have put down deposits of friendship, integrity, and care and concern with people, we can overcome adversity.

We had a situation on our basketball team that exemplified this. At the end of our season, while we were preparing for our conference tournament, two of our starting players had a fight. One was black and the other white, so it had the potential to divide our team racially. But when we got to the crux of the problem, it had nothing to do with race. It was a conflict between post and perimeter players. If the players had not put sufficient deposits in the bank, this adversity could have torn our team apart. Instead, once we got everything in the open, we became a closer, stronger team because a problem that had been festering for a while was now addressed and put to rest. We were fortunate to win the conference tournament and advance to the NAIA National Basketball Tournament that season. Deposits in the bank do allow teams to stare adversity in the face and beat it.

Former President Ronald Reagan had teamwork pretty well summed up when he told one of his favorite stories about two young men hiking in the mountains of northern California. As they were hiking, they came across the biggest grizzly bear either of them had ever seen. One fellow sat down and pulled a pair of running shoes from his backpack. His buddy asked if he thought those shoes would help him outrun the bear. His response was, "No, but they'll help me outrun you." I would not want that guy on my team!

To a great extent, teamwork begins with planning. The more inclusive the planning, the more we get everyone on the same page. Once everyone is on the same page, a great leader gets out of the way and allows his team to work. He has built an environment of trust; he trusts his team. When excellent results come to fruition, a great leader gives all the credit to the team. He gave them the responsibility and now he acknowledges, appreciates, and commends their work. Strong leaders build strong teams.

Consider:

Think about the importance of teamwork in your leadership style. Does it hold a preeminent position? Do you sincerely believe that you never know where the best ideas will come from? Do you strive to inculcate interdependence in your organization?

TOUGHNESS

Toughness enables you to handle critics and to demand excellence from your people. Leaders can also give the gift of toughness to their constituents.

We all know people who constantly complain. Nothing is ever good: their back hurts, their knees hurt, the weather is lousy. They are always whining and grumbling about their state in life. The second T is the antithesis of people who complain all day long. It stands for *toughness.* The tough-minded people I've worked with complain very little, because they are too busy doing. Sister Rosemary Small was a Franciscan nun with whom I worked for thirty years at the University of St Francis. She became wheelchair bound during her tenure with us. I have nothing but the highest regard for her and for her toughness. In all the years that I knew her, I never heard her complain.

I always liked the differentiation between managers and leaders. Managers try to do things right, but leaders try to do the right things. It's tough to do the right things. We once had to dismiss six players from a team at the College of St Francis. Obviously, we didn't want to be in this situation, because we had recruited these athletes and we cared about them. But due to their actions, we felt the right thing to do was to dismiss them. And many people weren't happy. When leaders try to do the right things, there is one outcome that they can be certain of: they will have critics.

Leaders have to be tough-minded when it comes to their critics. I think it helps to understand that all great leaders have had their critics. Dr. Martin Luther King Jr. had a great insight into critics when he began his "Letter from the Birmingham

Jail" by stating, "Seldom do I pause to answer criticism of my work and ideas. If I sought to answer all the criticisms that cross my desk, my secretaries would have little time for anything other than such correspondence in the course of the day, and I would have no time for constructive work." Father Theodore Hesburgh, president of the University of Notre Dame for twenty-six years, wrote an essay titled "College Presidency—Life Between a Rock and a Hard Place." He had the following insight into leadership and critics. For twenty-six years he did all he could to help his faculty—better benefits, better salaries, etc.—and through all these years, he received very few thank-you notes from faculty. However, when he made decisions that faculty did not agree with, his office was inundated with their letters.

Leaders cannot spend a great deal of time worrying about their critics. Maybe this unknown author had it figured out when he wrote "An Irishman's Philosophy," a good philosophy for leaders to consider:

There are only two things to worry about, you are either well or sick.

If you are well, there is nothing to worry about, but if you are sick, there are two things you have to worry about.

You will either get better or you will die.

If you're going to get better, there is nothing to worry about, but if you are going to die, there are two things you have to worry about.

You are either going to heaven or you are going to hell.

If you're going to heaven, there is nothing to worry about, but if you are going to hell, you will be so damn busy shaking hands with all your friends, you will not have time to worry.

Leaders will always have critics, and worrying about them will not make them go away.

Toughness has always been a major aspect of sports. Games are tough. Competition is tough. We always liked to hear our players tell recruits that our practices were harder than our games. We had to be demanding and tough on our players during practices to prepare them adequately for games.

Leaders have to understand that being demanding and tough with their employees, students, or teams is a good thing. Think about the best teacher you ever had. Think about the best coach you ever had. Would you say that teacher or that coach was easy on you? Or would you say he or she was demanding and tough? I believe most of us would say that teacher or coach was demanding. And it was precisely that leader's toughness that brought out the best in us. We may have reached levels that we didn't think we were capable of. The result was that we were proud of our accomplishments.

While in college, I had two teachers who were especially tough and demanding. One was in the academic realm and the other in the athletic arena. Brother Paul French of the De La Salle Christian Brothers order was an English professor who later became president of Lewis College. I had him for a class in Shakespeare that focused on the comedies and the history plays. We studied one play per week for the semester, and I never worked harder in any class than I did in that one. I also learned more in that class than any other class I ever had, including graduate courses. I came to have a genuine appreciation of Shakespeare, especially the depiction of his characters and his bawdy humor. I studied twenty hours for the final exam to prove to myself that I could earn an A in the most challenging class I'd ever had. Despite Brother Paul's demands, I actually felt bad that I couldn't take his Shakespeare tragedies class the next semester because the English Department assigned the tragedies to another professor. I wanted to study with the best teacher for the best of Shakespeare's writing. He was truly an extraordinary teacher.

Coaching is ultimately teaching, and I was blessed in college to have a coach, Gordie Gillespie, who was equally as extraordinary as Brother Paul. Gordie, who won his 1,800th baseball game at age eighty-two, was demanding. Our practices were tough, and he expected us to give our best effort every minute of those practices. He never stopped demanding our best effort, which is exemplified by the following story. I was pitching in a summer game; Gordie was coaching third base; and it was a very hot, humid night. It was the top of the ninth inning, and we had a big lead: something like 9–1. I was on first base with two outs. I had been pitching a good game, was a little tired, and had to get only three outs to get the win for us. A fly ball was hit right at the left fielder, and it was pretty obvious that it was going to be caught to end the inning. So, instead of running hard, in the event the left fielder might drop the ball, I pretty much trotted to second base. The inning was over, and as I crossed the field to get my glove to pitch the bottom of the ninth, I met Gordie. Now, I was fatigued, had pitched eight quality innings, and needed only the final three outs. And Gord said only five words: "Don't ever do that again."

It was not acceptable that I failed to run hard. Forget the heat, forget the game I was pitching, forget the fact that that ball was going to be caught 99 percent of the time. None of that mattered. Gordie always demanded your best effort; he demanded excellence and I had loafed on a play. I never have forgotten his reaction. Excellence was not to be a sometime thing.

Three friends have taught me what toughness is. My good friend and fellow coach with whom I worked for twenty-four years at the University of St. Francis, Jack Hermanski, is one of the toughest people I have ever met. Seventeen years ago, Jack was diagnosed with multiple sclerosis. Because he had taught special education for twenty-five years, he knew firsthand where this disease could lead.

Losing his vision and his ability to walk were just two of the pitfalls he might have to face in his future.

Jack had and has the toughness to meet MS head-on. He never complains, and he will absolutely not allow the disease to defeat him. Coach Jack and I still conduct shooting clinics. He teaches with a walker now, and his teaching is so good that as the clinic progresses you don't notice the walker. His toughness is a daily inspiration to me and to all who know him.

I worked with a great professor at the College of St. Francis, Dr. Jim McCabe. The students loved Mac, and he was highly respected by his fellow faculty members. I also coached a basketball player at the college, Pat Quigley, who earned the same respect as Jim. Quig's teammates, coaches, and the professors thought the world of him. He was everything you could possibly want in an athlete or a student. Jim and Pat showed me the meaning of extraordinary toughness at the most trying time of their lives. I was at the bedside of both of them days before they died. The great majority of our conversation was laughter, even at a time like this. How they found the courage to laugh, given their circumstances, I will never know. But laugh they did!

Leaders must accept that they will have critics and that the line may be a long one. In my second year as a head high school basketball coach, our timekeeper inadvertently let time slip away at the end of a game that we were winning. The opposing coach called the referees over and told them time had to be put back on the clock. The referees approached me, and I simply told them to put the time that they thought was fair. They did, and we went on to win.

After the game, a parent of one of our players came to me and criticized my allowing the referees to put time back on the clock. His rationale was that if we were on the road, time would never have been put back on the clock for us. My answer was that the players on the bench and the coaches knew the timekeeper had erred, and what kind of example would I be giving the kids if I argued about something that I knew was wrong. He didn't buy it, but that was okay. I did what I knew was right. All coaches want to win—we certainly are no exception to having that desire—but I always believed that we should win the right way. Time slippage occurred a few more times in my career, and my answer never changed - put the time back on the clock, and let's play.

While coaching during a game, I rarely heard the crowd, especially my plethora of critics in the stands. However, there was one exception. We were playing at the University of North Dakota, and their student section was sitting directly behind our bench. All night long, I heard the refrain, "Hey, Pat," followed by a humorous statement about my lousy coaching. Those kids were really creative. On one North Dakota free throw, I yelled to our players, "You big men, block-out!" The next thing I heard was, "Hey, Pat, you ain't got no big men!" Toward the end of the game there was a time-out; the gym was relatively quiet; and I heard, "Hey, Pat" again, followed by, "What junior high did you coach at last year?" The very end of the game was not fun at all, because we lost on an illegal, dead ball shot at the buzzer, but my critics that night had done a great job.

Gordie heard a vocal critic one night that he liked to quote. His Joliet Catholic High School football team was playing Chicago Mount Carmel. One fan was continuously ripping Gordie's coaching as the game progressed. Finally he came out with this unforgettable, erudite line: "Gordie, I'm leaving. These kids are playing like high school kids." Gord never forgot that one-liner.

Coaches will always have their critics, and I can honestly say they never bothered me. I always felt that if they came to our practices and heard and saw the game plan, they may not have understood half of what the players had to absorb. I believe coaches and leaders have a lot in common when it comes to our critics.

There is a final reason why a leader's toughness is good for the people he leads. The leader's toughness can make his people tough; if leaders give the gift of toughness to their people, they are truly giving them a lifelong gift. The title of retired televangelist, pastor, motivational speaker, and author Dr. Robert Schuller's best-selling book attests to this concept: *Tough Times Don't Last but Tough People Do*. Scott Peck begins his book *The Road Less Traveled* by stating, "Life is difficult." All the people we lead have either experienced tough times or they will. There is no question that there is a lot of adversity out there, and no one is exempt from it. Leaders who give the gift of toughness to the people they lead equip them with a great asset.

However, there must be a balance. I graduated from college in the "old days." We were told that when we entered that classroom as a teacher, we had to be so tough that we would not smile until Christmas. Teachers, coaches, and leaders have to be demanding. But it's okay to smile before Christmas. We must balance our toughness with kindness, care, and concern for those we lead beyond the narrow confines of a classroom, a football field, or a workplace. Once people know you genuinely care for them, they will understand and accept your rationale for demanding the best from them.

An anonymous author wrote the following about a smile:

A smile costs nothing, but it gives much.
It enriches those who receive, without making poorer those who give.
It takes but a moment, but the memory of it sometimes lasts forever.
It cannot be bought, begged, borrowed, or stolen for it is something that is of no value until it is given away.

Leaders must be tough and demanding, or the goals of their organization will not be reached. But at the same time, they must give away their smile and let their people know how much they care about their welfare. A classic representative of this tough/

compassionate integration was the former registrar at our university, Sister Margaret Duffy. The sign she had in her office let our students know they were walking into harm's way when they entered her office. It read, "What part of no don't you understand?" She could be tough on the students, but at the same time she loved them, and they loved her. Her enduring legacy of balancing toughness and compassion is best summed up by a sentence in a memorial published after her passing in December 2012 by the Sisters of St. Francis of Mary Immaculate: "She had a way of challenging the status quo with a blunt common sense approach to problems."

Leaders must develop tough-mindedness, or their critics can destroy them. They must also develop the toughness to demand, or I don't think their organization will ever reach excellence. If their demanding develops tough-mindedness in their people, they are giving a true gift to them that will enable them to meet adversity head-on. Smiles and humor can and should be integrated with the demands. Organizations can produce results and have fun doing it.

Consider:

Reflect on your tough-mindedness. Are you a demanding or an easy leader? Do you consciously try to balance your demands with empathy?

INTELLIGENCE

Developing listening skills and persevering in core values make for an intelligent leader.

Could this be possible? Of all people, a coach talking about intelligence! This has to be an oxymoron—a definitive contradiction of terms.

One of my favorite stories is about the football coach and the basketball coach who were sitting in the football coach's office talking about how dumb their players were. So they tried an experiment. The football coach called in his star player and asked him if he knew where the local Mercedes dealership was. The player said yes, so the coach gave him a twenty-dollar bill and asked him to go buy a car for him. The player quickly left the office so he could run his errand.

The basketball coach called in his star player and asked him if he knew where his office was. The athlete said, "Yes, it's upstairs." The coach asked, "Will you go up there and see if I'm up there?" The player said, "Sure."

On the way to their respective jobs, the two athletes met. The football player said to the basketball player, "My coach is really dumb. He gave me money to buy him a car but never once said what color car he wanted." The basketball player replied, "You think that's bad. My coach is sitting in your coach's office, asked me to go up to his office to see if he is up there, and all along there is a phone sitting right there—all he had to do was call."

I have never believed in the day of the dumb athlete and never will, and I resent those who promulgate this fallacy. There is so much to learn in all sports in terms of fundamentals and strategies that an athlete cannot be dumb and excel. There is no way this can happen.

Although I have spent forty-four years in education, and despite the fact that colleges and universities put so much emphasis on the ACT and SAT exams, I do not believe in those exams, because they cannot measure what is in a person's heart. They cannot measure desire and determination. And, some would argue, they cannot even measure intelligence accurately. So I do not believe these tests determine intelligence. But there are two characteristics that all the intelligent leaders that I've worked with or known have: a unique ability to listen and perseverance to their core values.

I worked with two highly intelligent leaders at the University of St Francis: President Jack Orr and Athletic Chairman and Baseball and Football Coach Gordie Gillespie. Both of them had an extraordinary ability to listen and were very much like CEOs in their work. In one study, when asked how they spent their time, the CEOs researched gave this breakdown:

10 percent—writing
15 percent—reading
30 percent—speaking
45 percent—listening

I once had dinner in New York with arguably the greatest basketball coach in college history, UCLA's

John Wooden, and a high school coach. Ironically, the high school coach did most of the talking, while John Wooden did the majority of the listening. I have yet to meet an intelligent person who was not a great listener.

One of the great lessons of athletics is that both players and coaches are given the opportunity to improve and enhance their listening skills. Players have to listen to coaches' instruction in an emotionally charged—and often a hostile—environment. If the instruction comes at a time-out, the players must also absorb the information in a very short time. Great coaches reciprocate. Like great leaders, they listen to their players' insights.

The first year that we became competitive at St. Francis in the Chicagoland Collegiate Athletic Conference, we were 9–2 and Chicago State University was 10–1. We had to play the last conference game at their place with the opportunity to tie for the championship if we could win. The game came down to the final two seconds; we were down two points and had an inbound under our basket. At the time-out, we drew up the play we were going to run. If one player failed to listen, the play would not work. So five months of hard work came down to two seconds, and listening was the key to execution. All the players did listen; we scored and took the game into overtime. We eventually lost the game in double overtime, but I could not have been prouder of how our players listened and played in that great basketball environment.

Coaches also listen to players. At Providence High School, we were playing Chicago Christian for the championship of the Chicago Private League. We both came into the game at 10–1. The game was tied with fifteen seconds to go. We had the ball and would get the last shot of the game. I told the players at the time-out the play we would run, directing them to get the ball inside to our post man from the wing. The players then offered me the insight that the better position to get the ball inside was from the point. I listened to them; the ball did get inside from the point; and we won the championship.

We had two delay games we would run at the end of games when we were in the lead. It was not uncommon for me to ask the players at a time-out which of the two they wanted to run. They were playing the game, and they had a feel for the game, so I would give them ownership of the decision. We did the same with post defense. We guarded the post three different ways. There were times when I would ask the kids which one they wanted to use. They were in the trenches, and I trusted their decisions.

Gordie used the Socratic teaching method at halftimes of Joliet Catholic High School football games. His halftimes were question-and-answer periods. He would assemble his offensive unit in the locker room, call out one of the plays they had run in the first half, and then ask the players how the opponents were defending it. They would answer the questions, and from their answers Gordie would make adjustments for the second half. I often listened to these exchanges and came away so proud of the kids' intelligence and Gordie's willingness to listen. I once brought former Utah basketball coach, Rick Majerus, into one of these sessions. After we left the locker room, I asked Rick what he thought. He said, "It was sure different from the halftimes I remember in high school, where the coaches cussed at us and questioned our gender."

The best athletic listening episode I ever had was during a halftime of a game against McKendree College. Our locker room was in the corner of their gym, right next to the outside sidewalk. We had a very good team that year and had just played a poor first half. I was pretty upset and got to yelling at the kids pretty loudly—so loudly that when I asked the players, "How can we possibly be playing like this!" from outside the building we heard, "Because we're better than you!" That stopped my ranting and raving right in its tracks. I may have thought I was a pretty good listener as a coach, but that was the only time I listened to a comment from outside a building. We did play a great second half; maybe the ole boy outside the gym fired our guys up. And we won the game, something that rarely happened at McKendree.

I have never understood leaders who don't pay attention to the people in the trenches, the people who are doing the work. Why would you make decisions without input from the people doing the job? I'll never forget what happened while I was working ironworking one summer. The ironworkers I was working with were experienced in the trade and very intelligent. I thought it was great that the architects would come to the job and ask questions of these men. The architects were drawing up the plans, but they checked with the men in the trenches to ascertain if what they were designing would work. They listened intently to the advice of those ironworkers. That was high-quality leadership.

Dr. Jack Orr, as previously noted, led St. Francis to national respectability. After his retirement, I asked him why he thought his tenure was so successful. His answer was different from mine; he said attention to detail. He definitely did that, but I thought his greatest asset was his ability and his willingness to listen.

The second characteristic of the intelligent people I have met is perseverance to their core values. This trait also fits some of the greatest minds in history. Thomas Edison was said to have tried ten thousand experiments before developing the first practical incandescent electric light. When asked why he kept trying in the midst of perpetual failure, his answer was reported to be, "Because now I know ten thousand ways that it won't work." I don't know what Thomas Edison would have scored on the ACT or the SAT, but I sure know he had perseverance.

When Winston Churchill flunked sixth grade, the teacher wrote that he was "dumb and hopeless." Thank God he didn't buy into that assessment; he persevered to become one of the greatest leaders of the twentieth century. Or how about the man who was told he was wasting his time drawing—Walt Disney. History agrees it's a good thing he kept drawing. How could a deaf man pursue music? If he hadn't persevered the world never would have known Beethoven.

Two men from my hometown of Joliet, Illinois, also exhibited perseverance. One was Daniel "Rudy" Ruettiger, on whose life the movie *Rudy* is based. Rudy graduated third from the bottom of his high school class. After serving in the Navy, he told people in town that he was going to Notre Dame, and they laughed. No one believed there was any way he could ever be admitted to Notre Dame. When he said he was going to play football there, the laughter grew louder. No one believed a five-foot-eight, 180-pound athlete would ever get on a Notre Dame football roster.

But against all odds, Rudy accomplished both goals, and because of his great perseverance he travels the country today encouraging America's youth never to give up on their dreams. He has been an inspiration to thousands of our young people.

My brother, Dan, was a good friend of Rudy's. Like Rudy, he too graduated close to the bottom of his high school class. But he persevered through college and became an outstanding high school teacher and coach. He finished his career as a principal and has had a very positive influence on countless young people.

I certainly saw perseverance to core values one night in a game at Chicago State University. They were ranked nationally and had a guard on their team named Dave Maracich, a very good player. His dad, Ed, was a respected, long-time Big Ten football and basketball official. I have always believed that the primary core value of referees is that they want to make the right call. We were in a very close game with Chicago State, and I disagreed with a call, feeling we should have been awarded a free throw. I approached the officials on it, and they listened. Then they went to midcourt to talk it over. While they were conferring at midcourt, I happened to look in the stands, where Ed was giving the referees the shooting signal. He wanted the right call, even though it went against his son's team in a close game. We shot the free throw.

Gordie had a similar incident in a baseball game. The umpire made a call that favored Gordie's team. The opposing coach went to the umpire to question the call. After a short discussion, the umpire reversed the call, thus hurting Gordie's team. Gord then went to the umpire to argue with him for changing his mind. As he approached him to chastise him for reversing his call, the umpire said, "Do you want me not to change my mind and make the wrong call or to change my mind and make the right call." Gordie finished the story by saying he immediately turned around and went back to the dugout.

I think former Joliet Bishop Romeo Blanchette made the right call when he vetoed his own committee and kept Providence High School open. I have no idea why he made the call, but I often wondered if it was because his core values centered on the Catholic Church's role to serve all people. At the time of his decision, I believe Providence may have been the only school in the diocese that had a diverse enrollment. Hispanic and African American students attended there, and we also served white kids who came from the poorer neighborhoods in Joliet, the east and south sides. I have always thought that Bishop Blanchette's core values were the centerpiece of his controversial and courageous decision to veto his own committee.

I have been fortunate to direct basketball clinics throughout America where some of the best coaches in the country have presented: John Wooden, Dean Smith, Bob Knight, Hubie Brown—all of them were great leaders. The one trait I observed in each of them was their ability to listen.

The movie *Rudy* is a testament to perseverance to core values. I think the only person who ever thought Rudy would be admitted, let alone graduate and play football at Notre Dame, was Rudy. He was truly a majority of one. I believe listening may be the most important skill a leader can develop, and especially during tough times, a leader must stay strong in his or her core values.

Consider:

Reflect on the two characteristics that make up an intelligent leader. Do you listen to your people? Do you value the opinion of everyone in your organization? Have you ever put your core values in writing? When the tough times have come to your organization, have you relied on these values?

THANK-YOU

**Thanking and complimenting ALL
your people goes a long way.**

In their outstanding book about corporate America, *In Search of Excellence*, authors Thomas J. Peters and Robert H. Waterman speak about a very simple concept that top executives in companies— vice presidents, presidents, and CEOs— very seldom say to the people who are making the company successful, such as secretaries, truck drivers, assembly-line workers. That simple yet profound concept is the third T of ATTITUDE: Thank-You.

It's a simple theory for leaders. You must demand to get production, but when workers meet the demands and achieve their goals, you must compliment and thank them for their efforts.

There is also merit to thanking the people who are seldom recognized. In my coaching career, I grew to have more respect for the players on the bench than the starters and the stars. When we were having good years, many people on campus were patting the starters on the back and congratulating them on the season we were having. But those very same campus people may not have even known that the kids on the bench were on the team. However, it was those athletes who were so instrumental in our having that great season. They were the athletes who were there every day, making the starters better players, despite the fact that they were getting little or no recognition for their efforts. So I made it a priority to compliment and thank them for their work. As their leader, I wanted to be sure they knew how much I appreciated all they were doing for our team.

Al McGuire, the former Marquette basketball coach, said he never worried about the last men on the team, the players on the bench, because when they were in their forties they were top executives in companies. But he did worry about the stars, because when they were in their forties, no one was carrying their bags and telling them how wonderful they were.

We found this to be true at St Francis. A number of our players who didn't receive the playing time they wanted have gone on to top positions in companies. They are also among the top financial contributors to our university. The old adage about hiring offensive linemen is analogous to the players on the bench. Both of these athletes do all their work for virtually no recognition. But they do know how to roll up their sleeves and get to work. They become MVPs in their companies.

I know firsthand how much a thank-you is appreciated. Years ago I started my "Keeper's Drawer," where I keep thank-you and congratulatory letters that I have received. Ironically, I have kept them in that drawer for years, but I have never taken the time to just sit and read through them. A number of them have come from my children and former players. I think thank-yous confirm what you have tried to do in your life's work and how you have tried to be of service. Very few of us who chose education as a profession will be among the top 1 percent financially. However, when the thank-you letters come, you do feel like you have made a contribution. Some rainy day I'm going to that drawer and do a little belated reading.

Given the above, when I speak at athletic banquets or to any youth groups, I do ask the young people to consider writing a thank-you note to a teacher or coach who inspired them. I know that coach or teacher would appreciate the letter. I then ask them to give strong consideration to doing the same for their parents. All of us who have participated in sports know or should know the many sacrifices our parents have made to give us these opportunities. Heating and reheating of dinner, picking us up at all hours of the day and night from practices, attendance at so many games, often traveling great distances—these are only some of the sacrifices our parents have made. It would seem that a thank-you note to them is not asking too much.

However, I follow that request by saying to parents that if that letter never arrives, they can turn to the wisdom of Mark Twain. He had a good insight into youth when he wrote, "When I was fourteen, I couldn't believe how dumb my old man was. Then when I turned twenty-one, I couldn't believe how much the old man learned in those seven years."

When I speak to business leaders, I also encourage them to consider thanking a former teacher or coach who positively influenced them. A thank-you from someone working in their profession, someone older who has a bit of life behind him or her, is even more important, more gratifying. But the main people I ask them to consider thanking are those not normally recognized. So many people give so much to an organization and are never recognized. At the college level, some faculty look down on the maintenance staff. How wrong they are! Were it not for the maintenance men and women keeping the college presentable, faculty would have no students to teach. Everyone contributes, and great leaders appreciate and thank everyone in the organization.

At the College of St. Francis, our primary source of income was tuition from our students. One of the many things I admired about our president, Dr. Jack Orr, was how welcome he made our students feel. Unlike so many presidents, he actually knew our students. It wasn't uncommon for Jack to join students at their cafeteria table for lunch. Three of our alums, Randy Stelter, Mike Brennan, and Ron Kenny have often told me how surprised they were and how much they appreciated the fact that the president of the college took the time to sit with them at lunch. He knew their names then, and when they returned later for alumni events, he still called them by name. Mike told me that, in his work in the world of high finance, he often works with men and women who are graduates of large, prestigious universities. As they get talking about their collegiate years, Mike would say, "Yes, you went to a great university, but I'll bet your president never joined you for lunch."

Jack took his concern for our students a step further. I was once at the wake of a wonderful teacher-coach I worked with for over a decade. When Jack walked into the wake, I was very surprised, because I didn't think he knew the coach. It turned out that he didn't know him, but because his daughter was a student at St. Francis, he attended the wake. I believe he did this for a number of our students when they lost a parent.

Jack truly knew how to thank those students who came to St. Francis. He knew them when they were students; he remembered them when they became alums; and he was there for them in their most trying times. That is a leader who knows how to say thanks.

Now, in our day, growing up, there wasn't a lot of political correctness, and we rarely heard thank-you from our leaders. We had a tough, cantankerous, older priest as the pastor of our parish church. Because we lived across the street from our church, my brother, Dan, and I often served 6:30 a.m. daily Mass. You would think our pastor would have appreciated our efforts. A number of times he sarcastically chastised me for making altar boy errors, but he topped his list of "thank-yous" when he said to Dan, "Sullivan, I have been a priest for forty-five years, and you are the dumbest altar boy I have ever seen!"

We were on a family vacation in the Ozarks when we saw a sign reading "Abundant Memories." In the valley below the road were about seven individual cabins. We had no idea what was down there, but we decided to explore it. We were met by a man with a long beard and bib overalls. He told us he had traveled over two hundred thousand miles throughout our country, acquiring various artifacts that represented different eras in American history. He then gave my children and me the best history class we've ever had.

Each cabin represented a time in our history—Revolutionary War, Civil War, the Depression, etc.—and in each cabin he had artifacts from that period. As we moved from cabin to cabin, he lectured on each period by using the artifacts to explain the highpoints of that time in our history. I have never forgotten his points on the Civil War. He explained to us that at the end of the war, our government was broke. So President Lincoln, not able to pay the soldiers, gave them land.

Then he picked a tool from that period and said some people would call it "primitive." But he said he would call it "ingenious" and then proceeded to show us all that could be done with the tool. His final statement, while holding the tool in his hands, was that the politicians and the wealthy did not build this country. He said the "nobodies" built this country. That comment made me think of the kids at the end of the bench, the offensive linemen, and my father.

My dad was a nobody in the eyes of the world. He grew up in the Depression and had to go to work to help his family when he finished the sixth grade. He worked in factories all his life and had no title behind his name—not doctor, lawyer, or teacher. But I can say without equivocation that during my thirty-four years in higher education, I have yet to meet a person with a doctorate who had the wisdom of my dad.

I think it's especially important for leaders to thank the people they lead and to give strong consideration to thanking the "nobodies."

In the fourteenth century, German philosopher Meister Eckhart wrote something that succinctly covers this thank-you concept: "If the only prayer you ever say in your entire life is 'thank-you,' it will be enough." I have tried to make this my primary prayer, because there is so much to be thankful for.

Leaders know or should know they can't achieve success in their organization by themselves. You simply can't get it done alone. You want everyone under your purview to be outstanding at his or her job, regardless of how big or small that person's responsibilities may be. Everyone plays a part in the team's success, and it is important that the leader recognizes everyone's contributions with a simple, heartfelt **THANK-YOU**!

Consider:

Think about the importance of "thank-you." Do you appreciate it when people thank you for whatever you may have done for them? How often have you thanked your people for the effort they bring to your organization? Have you recognized and thanked the "nobodies?"

YOU

Your work ethic leads to your success; great leaders surround themselves with great people; and quality leaders do all they can to help others.

The best definition of a teacher, a coach, or a leader that I have ever heard is a one- word definition. That word is *facilitator*. Great teachers, coaches, and leaders facilitate learning. They make learning easier.

Think about the best teacher, coach, or leader you have ever known. Did he or she exemplify these four things?

1. **Knowledgeable:** They knew their subject matter, be it geometry, football, or a particular business. John Wooden, at sixty-five years of age and the most successful tournament coach in NCAA basketball history, used to tell his players how much he was still learning about the game. Great leaders are lifelong learners.

2. **Organized:** They were organized in their presentations and therefore could disseminate their knowledge. Many of us have known brilliant professors who simply could not bring their knowledge down to us mortals, to our level. They definitely had the knowledge but could not disseminate it.

3. **Enthusiastic:** They taught, coached, or led with enthusiasm. I am not referring to "rah, rah" enthusiasm, but rather being excited about our achievements. They loved what they were doing but they

were especially happy when we took their knowledge and achieved success.

4. **Caring:** Most importantly, they cared about us beyond the narrow confines of the classroom, the athletic arena, or the workplace. I thought the best example of this in coaching was Amos Alonzo Stagg, the former football coach at the University of Chicago, when they were members of the Big Ten Conference. His degree from Yale University was in divinity, but he felt he could better minister to America's youth from a football field than a pulpit.

The greatest teachers, coaches, and leaders, I believe, do the above four things. But I also believe this: it makes no difference how outstanding those teachers, coaches, and leaders are, because they can't make you learn. The only person who can make you learn is **YOU.** I do believe we have gotten away from that concept in America today. We are awful quick to blame that teacher, coach, or leader when we should be looking in the mirror.

I have coached All-Conference, All-State, and All-American players, and I know one thing for sure: I never made any one of them a player. The only one who made them into the quality players they became was themselves. Their work in the off-season, their work in the weight room, and their daily work at practice were what led to their excellence. I may have facilitated a little of their learning; but they, and only they, put in the time and effort to excel.

Education has changed during my forty-four years in the field. I offer two examples of the change from responsibility and accountability to too much irresponsibility and unaccountability. During my first day of high school classes, I was asked the square root of a number in my algebra class. I was sitting in the last seat of the middle row, stood up, and told the priest I didn't know. As I was standing there, the priest got up from behind his desk and started walking toward me. I had heard that the teachers at this school could be tough on you, so I was a little apprehensive. He was rubbing his hands in front of him as he was coming toward me, and he said when I come into his class, I'd better know. He finished his walk by smacking me in the head.

Now, please don't get me wrong. I'm not saying corporal punishment is necessary. I don't believe we need it to learn. On the other hand, I disagree with what happened to a teacher friend of mine a number of years ago. A high school kid called him the worst cuss word in the English language, so my friend decided to take him to the school dean and report the incident. The dean's first question was to the teacher, not the student. He asked what he, the teacher, had done to precipitate the student's behavior. That was the last time my friend went to the dean. The smack in the head was neither right nor necessary, but the dean's reaction may have been worse. When we don't make students responsible for their actions, I don't think we are educating them.

I think the "you" in the attitude acronym has two implications for leaders.

If education has changed and if some students are not accepting responsibility for their actions, leaders must take a great deal of time in the hiring stage to find the responsible ones. They are definitely out there. I have encountered a lot more responsible kids than irresponsible ones in my teaching and coaching career, but leaders must take the time to find them.

Great leaders want to surround themselves with quality people. I believe every successful leader has good people around him or her. I think Andrew Carnegie, a billionaire in the steel business, best summed up this concept when he said that if he had to make steel, he would probably be a pauper, because he didn't know how to make it. If he had to sell steel, again he might be a pauper, because he didn't know how to sell it. However, he said what he could do was find the best people who knew how to make it and the best people who knew how to sell it and he could get them in a room and have them work together. So, you, the leader, want to find people like you—people who are motivated to be the best they can be.

There is another side to "you," and Albert Einstein addressed this important aspect when he told a *New York Times* reporter on June 20, 1932, "Only a life lived for others is a life worthwhile." In the last analysis, I don't think it's about you; but it is about you helping others. When I do start to think it is "about me" and "how great I am," I reflect on the highlights of my athletic career.

One of my former college players, Tom Denny, became the head basketball coach at my alma mater, Joliet Catholic High School, and informed me that I was in the school's basketball record book. I was pretty proud of myself until he told me why I was in this prestigious book: "You committed the fourth most fouls in the history of Joliet Catholic basketball."

Between my junior and senior years of college, there was a renowned baseball tournament that attracted the best teams in our area. One of the local teams added me to their roster for this tournament. They felt I was a good pitcher and could help them win the championship. But they realized they had bad judgment after the very first batter. There were no fences on this field, and left field sloped as you moved away from the field. That first batter hit the ball so far over the left fielder's head that he disappeared from sight as he chased the ball. The batter could have circled the bases three times. So much for my pitching prowess!

My basketball expertise was probably best summed up by one of my high school coaches, Jim Gannon. In my playing days, you hardly heard of concussions. But I am sure I got one in a game at Marmion Military Academy. I took three hits—hard hits—to the head. I was definitely quite hazy for a good portion of the game. Coach Gannon summed up my basketball ability and the way concussions were handled in our day when he told me after the game, "Sullivan, you play better when you don't know where you are!"

Finally, I was the hero. We had a basketball game that went into two overtimes. In our day, the rule after two overtimes was that the game would go to what was called "sudden death." It meant that the first team with a two-point lead won the game. We secured the jump ball, and I went off two screens and made the game-winning shot. After the game, we had a dance in our gym. At our dances, the girls danced on the basketball floor and the boys walked around the periphery trying to garner the courage to ask one of the girls to dance. Toward the end of the evening, I found the courage to ask one of the girls. Her answer was pretty definitive. She looked at me and simply said no. Even when I was the hero, I couldn't get a dance.

So whenever I think it's about me, I recall the above incidents and thank God it isn't about me. What it is about is leaders helping others. We have a great example of this in Morris, Illinois. Joe Schmitz is a former bank executive who spends his retirement time as the leader of Operation St. Nick. Joe and his committee identify needy families in

Grundy County who do not have the money to buy Christmas gifts for their children. He spends the year raising money so he can help these families purchase clothes, toys, and food for their family.

For Christmas 2012, Joe led his team in raising $83,000 to help these families, especially the children, have a blessed Christmas. They helped seventy-seven families with 171 children, spending $28,000 on food, $35,000 on toys, clothes, and gifts, and $20,000 on honorably discharged military families. He began Operation St. Nick thirty years ago and has helped countless families truly enjoy Christmas. Joe may be the best example I know of a leader extending himself to help others. And it is never about Joe; it's about the families he's helping.

As I look back on my life, I realize how fortunate I've been to have mentors who exemplified the four characteristics I cited previously that great teachers, coaches, and leaders have: knowledge, organization, enthusiasm, and caring.

Gordie Gillespie and Dr. Jack Orr surely knew their subject matter. Gordie was such a great collegiate basketball coach at Lewis College that there was a point when we thought he was going to be named the Marquette University basketball coach. The Chicago Cubs offered him the position to run their entire minor league system, from Rookie ball to Triple A. They wanted to get conformity of teaching throughout their system, and they believed Gordie was the best man to accomplish that goal.

Pat Mudron and Tom Thayer were outstanding football players who played for Gordie in high school and went on to play at the University of Notre Dame. Tom also had a great NFL career, including starting on the Chicago Bears Super Bowl championship team. I have heard both Tom and Pat say they thought Gordie would have been the ideal Notre Dame football coach. It's almost incomprehensible that a coach could ever be that superb in three sports. How blessed was I to play for and later work with Gordie for over two decades! You couldn't find a better mentor in terms of athletic knowledge.

Jack Orr was president of the College of St. Francis when collegiate accrediting agencies were very skeptical of colleges sponsoring academic programs off-campus. During all this skepticism, Jack brought St. Francis into nineteen states. So we could have been a prime target for off-campus academic criticism. Instead the North Central Accrediting Agency asked Jack to speak to his fellow presidents on quality in off-campus programs. Both Gordie and Jack knew their subject matter as well as anyone in their respective professions, and I was extremely fortunate to serve under their leadership.

I studied in college under a professor who knew his subject matter and could disseminate his knowledge. Brother Phillip Lynch taught Rhetoric and Composition and Speech at Lewis College. His knowledge resonates with me and some friends who studied under him to this day. And that was over forty years ago! George and Frank Black are two very successful lawyers in Morris, Illinois, and it seems like every time we meet, we eventually get around to talking about the excellent teaching of Brother Phillip.

Enthusiasm for teaching was certainly exemplified by Tom Dedin. Tom was my first athletic director and, in my opinion, the best classroom teacher at Providence High School during our years there. He also became the head baseball coach at Lewis College, then the University of Illinois. He was a great mentor for me and all his coaches because he demanded that we excel in the classroom. Coaches love teaching their respective sports. Tom wanted that, but never at the expense of their classroom teaching. He didn't have to tell us this; he taught it by example.

I was blessed to have numerous coaches, teachers, and leaders whom I knew cared about me beyond the academic realm, the athletic arena, and the workplace. Jim Gannon, one of my high school coaches, tried to get an athletic scholarship for me to his alma mater, Arkansas State University. Bishop Roger Kaffer was always present for the tough times in my life, like my father's passing. I had no idea he was going to concelebrate the Mass. Gordie Gillespie, while coaching three sports and teaching at the high school and collegiate levels, always found time to help me and my teammates. That attitude never changed in the twenty-five years I worked with him. Jack Orr was the same as Gordie in his care and concern for the students and staff at St. Francis. I could continue this list for quite some time, because I've worked with so many leaders who genuinely cared about the people they served.

I have truly been blessed to study under and work with people who did the four things great coaches, teachers, and leaders do. They knew their subject matter; they could disseminate their knowledge; they taught, coached, and worked with enthusiasm; and, most importantly, they cared about the people they were serving.

When it was my turn to lead, I was most fortunate to be surrounded by great people—not good people, but great people. Our coaches at St. Francis took our athletic program from forty-five student-athletes in our first year there to 377 at our zenith. We graduated 92 percent of our senior student-athletes over a twenty-year period. When our Chicagoland Collegiate Athletic Conference sent ninety teams to NAIA national championship play, one school, St. Francis, sent sixty of those ninety teams. That is how great our people were.

I was equally as fortunate as the head basketball coach at Providence High School and the College, later the University, of St. Francis. Mike Slovick, Dick Keto, Frank Palmasani, my brother, Dan, and Jaime Garcia were outstanding assistant coaches at Providence who went on to have very successful coaching careers. Bob Hoppenstead, Frank Kaufman, Walt Leuder, Mike Kress, Eric Long, Elgin Thompson, Jeff Bonebrake, Mike Zaworski , Jeff Mersereau, Cyril Nichols, DeMario Edwards, Dean Quarino, Bill Karavitas, Randy Stelter, Joe Kuhn, Dennis Hansen, and Mike Nuesteadt were superb assistants at St. Francis.

John Cornelius and Jack Hermanski were the absolute best. Both worked at local high schools, so their work at St. Francis was a part-time job. John gave us fourteen years and Jack twenty-four. We were a part-time job to which they gave full-time hours for minimal stipends. They were not only great teachers and coaches, they were also true friends of mine and my family. I could never put into words the gratitude I have for them. As John used to say, "The main job of an assistant coach is to keep the head coach sane." In my case, that was a pretty tall order! If leaders are to succeed, they must have men like John and Jack on their team.

I think there are two facets to the word *you* for leaders. You are responsible for your body of work. There are no shortcuts to excellence. You must be willing to put in the time and effort it takes to be successful, and you must surround yourself with people like you—people motivated to learn and to work. The second facet of *you* is once you achieve a position of leadership, you want to do all you can to help others just as other leaders were there to help you in your journey.

Consider:

Examine your body of work. Do you take responsibility for your actions? Have you surrounded yourself with outstanding people who will challenge you and make you grow? Do you take time to help others as you grow your organization?

DETERMINATION

Nothing great is accomplished
without great determination and a
strong FQ.

I was directing a basketball clinic in Salt Lake City, Utah, when Dale Brown, the former Louisiana State University coach, spoke about the most poignant concept I have ever heard in my years of coaching and teaching. If there is a theme to this book, it would be what he said that day:

Your FQ is more important than your IQ.

Your FQ is your failure quotient. How often can you fail at something and have the resiliency to get back up? Jackie Robinson got back up daily. Winston Churchill did not buy into being "dumb and hopeless." Rudy got back up both in the classroom and on the football field. My brother, Dan, became a principal despite twelve years of very difficult educational experiences.

This man may have had the strongest FQ in American history because his failures were so public:

> '31—He failed in business.
> '32—He ran for the Illinois legislature and lost. He also lost his job and was rejected for law school.
> '33—He borrowed money to start a business only to go bankrupt by the year's end.
> '36—He had a total nervous breakdown.
> '38—He sought the speaker position in the Illinois legislature and lost.

'40—He sought the elector position in the Illinois legislature and lost.

'43—He ran for US Congress and lost.

'46—He ran for Congress and won.

'48—He ran for reelection to Congress and lost.

'54—He ran for the US Senate and lost.

'56—He sought the vice presidential nomination of his party and lost.

Despite all these reported failures, in 1860 Abraham Lincoln was elected president of the United States.

Pat Riley, a former Los Angeles Lakers coach and current president of the Miami Heat, addressed the importance of a strong FQ when he wrote, "Success is getting up one more time than you have been knocked down."

Green Bay's Vince Lombardi also believed in the importance of a strong FQ when he wrote, "The greatest accomplishment is not in never falling, but in rising again after you fall."

In athletics we fail often. A very good hitter in baseball or softball fails seven of ten at bats. That is a 70 percent failure rate! An outstanding three-point shooter in basketball fails six of every ten attempts. Coaches work very hard on their preparation for games. "The Five Ps" are a mantra for many coaches: "Proper Preparation Prevents Poor

Performance." But often we have some of the best preparation, only to lose the game.

So how do you deal with failure? How do you develop a strong FQ? In his book *Taking It to the Limit*, Stan Kellner wrote that the field of cybernetics teaches two ways to meet failure:

Learn from it.
Put it behind you.

Learning from failure, both personal and professional, is the easy part. Putting it behind you is the tough part. A coaching friend talked about visualizing a big box behind you with a huge lock on it. We take the failure, put it in that box, and lock it up. Then we move on.

My FQ demands that I make a basket someday in Niles, Illinois. During my junior year in high school, we played Notre Dame of Niles in a conference basketball game. I took ten shots that night and made no baskets. We visited them again in my senior year, and I replicated that feat. Ten shots, not one basket. So I vowed that someday I was going to put a basketball in my car trunk, drive to Niles, find an outdoor basketball court, make **ONE** basket, and come home.

My coaching buddy, Jack Hermanski, reminded me of my play in Niles on a regular basis. Jack and I have conducted shooting camps for over twenty-five years. Whenever a boy or girl fails to make a basket in a shooting contest, Jack tells them, to make them feel better, "Go ask Coach Pat about Niles." I can't tell you the number of times I recounted that story.

Through the years, I saw so many examples of determination in athletes I played with or coached. Pat Warren was only a sometime starter on our high school baseball team. He went on to become an All-Conference player at one of the best collegiate baseball programs in America, the University of Miami. After his career there, he signed professionally with the Houston Astros.

Ed Spiezio, while playing college baseball at Lewis College, would ask our coach, Gordie Gillespie, for the covers of the baseballs when they were knocked off during practices. He would then fill them with socks to the size of a baseball, sew them up, and have his father or friends get about twenty feet from him, about a third of the distance of the pitcher's mound to home plate, and throw pitches to him as fast as they could. Ed was the best hitter I have ever seen in our area and, as noted earlier, went on to have a fine major league career with the Cardinals, Padres, and White Sox.

When Pat Quigley decided to join our basketball team at the College of St. Francis, both his high school coach, Mike Gillespie, and I didn't know if he would ever get playing time. We knew he would be an outstanding student and a great representative of our college, but we didn't know if he had the ability to play at our level. So much for our knowledge! All he did was lead us to the conference championship game in his junior year and become a unanimous All-Conference player. The university basketball court is now "Pat Quigley Court" due to the efforts of two of his teammates, Ron Kenny and Mike Brennan. Ron and Mike had great respect and love for Quigs and wanted his legacy continued at St. Francis. How blessed we were to have Pat choose our college, and how blessed Pat was to have teammates like Ron and Mike.

Pat's friend Dave Shea followed him to St. Francis. Dave was six-four, 156 pounds coming out of high school. We told him he obviously had to get stronger and probably would not play until his junior year. Again, our prognosis wasn't very good—thankfully. He became an All-Conference player his sophomore year, repeated in both his junior and senior years, and also was All-District his senior year. All-District meant Dave was among the top ten players in the twenty-one NAIA colleges and universities in the state of Illinois. He finished his fine collegiate career scoring over one thousand points.

My good friend Tom Kennedy went to Lewis College as a baseball player. When our coach, Gordie Gillespie, saw Tom play basketball, he asked him to come out for the team. This was quite unusual, because Tom didn't play high school basketball—not one game of high school basketball. Tom became a first-team All-American and was drafted by the Chicago Zephyrs, which is today's Washington Wizards NBA franchise. To this day he remains one of the best players ever to play at Lewis.

Scott Pekol was similar to Tom. He played only two years—freshman and sophomore—of high school basketball. He came to St. Francis and became an outstanding collegiate player. After his senior year, he attended a camp for basketball players looking to play in Europe. Tom Hehir, a coach from Limerick, Ireland, watched Scott outplay three six-foot-eleven NCAA Division I players and told us Scott was "the talk of the camp." Tom said he could get Scott a professional contract for a team in London.

These athletes represent a small sample of the players I have been connected with who exhibited great determination in their athletic careers. If I had the space, I could tell the stories of so many more determined players.

I have also seen the determination of many teams. The first year we had the opportunity to make the District 20 playoffs at St. Francis, we experienced an unbelievable loss. Only six of the twenty-one schools in Illinois made the playoffs, and we were right there to be one of the six if we could win our last game. We were down twelve points with about six minutes to play at McKendree College. We had a great run, and with two seconds left, we made two free throws to go up by one point. They inbounded to a player at our free throw line.

I naturally thought we had the game won as their player was some seventy-nine feet away from their basket and you surely don't score from there. Their player threw a baseball pass at their rim as time expired. And I don't believe it touched the rim. It went right in! We were officially out of the playoffs and had a five-hour van ride home to replay that shot. Being a former baseball pitcher, I went into our gym the next week, stood at the free throw line and wondered if I threw one hundred balls at the basket from that distance would even one go in. I thought it unlikely. Losing that way made our players determined to make the playoffs the next year, and we did.

I always felt our players at St. Francis were motivated, determined players just to come to us. For our first eleven years there, we had no gym. We practiced and played in a local armory. The toughest part of having that venue as our home court was the scarcity of heat. I can remember a referee once coming out for the second half with his parka on. One day at practice I yelled at one of our players, Larry Fitzgerald, "Fitz, will you please catch the ball!" He responded honestly, saying, "I can't. My hands are freezing." The next day we brought a thermometer into the gym. It was fifty-four degrees. Fitz was right. Despite those conditions, our players were determined to be the best they could be, and we did have some very good teams during those eleven years.

Dick Fassino was an incredible man from our neighborhood who worked with us as a volunteer coach. Dick made you determined. He accepted nothing but your best effort. For the Little League organization in our city, he took only kids from our neighborhood. He was so dedicated that on the nights we didn't have a game, he always held practices in the afternoon. I believe we practiced more than any other team in the league, and it showed in our championship play.

Dick also coached us in basketball at Sacred Heart grammar school. We had no gym and had some practices outside in our winter boots, after shoveling the snow off the court. Dick had a creative way of looking at our outside practices. He would tell us, "When we get in the gym for games and replace our boots with gym shoes, we will jump much higher than our opponents." Dick gave us so much of his time as a volunteer coach, and because of his efforts, a number of us were fortunate to go on to play high school and collegiate athletics.

I will never forget a radio interview before a Christmas tournament championship game at Hillsdale College in Hillsdale, Michigan. It was a four-team tournament, and we won our first game by ten points, while Hillsdale won theirs by forty. They had finished third in the nation the year before, returned four starters, and had a Division I outstanding player transfer to them. I believe they were 10–1 at the time and ranked in the top five in the nation.

Prior to the game, with a packed crowd in attendance, their radio announcer asked me in a pregame interview how it felt to be in such an intimidating environment—great Hillsdale team, sellout crowd, boisterous fans so loud you could hardly hear. Well, that made me mad. What were we, chopped liver? So I asked him if he'd ever heard of Chicago State University. Did he ever hear of Quincy College? Both were perennially nationally ranked teams, like Hillsdale. He said that he knew them, so I said, "We play those teams, and we're glad to be here. We really enjoy atmospheres like this." And I meant it. You're always glad to be in championship play with a packed gym. That interview, which I related to our players, made us more determined. We won by twenty-six in one of the greatest games I ever saw our kids play.

We took a trip to the West Coast to play two NCAA Division I teams, the University of San Francisco and Fresno State University. It was pretty special to practice in the San Francisco gym the night before the game and to see those two NCAA championship banners and the retired numbers of Bill Russell, K. C. Jones, and Bill Cartwright on their walls. And there we were—a school that nobody had heard of trying to get ready to play them. But our kids were determined. We played superbly, beat them by a point, and were quite surprised when a number of NBA scouts came to our locker room while I was in the press conference to talk to Coach Jack about how much they enjoyed watching our team play.

Determination and especially getting up from failure, from losing, are such a great part of athletics. I always felt the most important practices of the year were the ones after a loss. Players and coaches are naturally disappointed and down from a loss, but you have to have the resiliency to get back up. Developing a strong FQ may be the single greatest lesson of sport that can be carried into athletes' personal and professional lives.

The above examples come primarily from the world of athletics because determination plays such an important role in sport. But determination certainly transcends athletics. I think all success, regardless of the field—medicine, law, business, education—begins with a leader's determination, which includes a strong FQ. Very few successes have not experienced failure along the way. Some things cannot be *taught*, but they can be *caught*. A leader's determination can be caught and infused throughout an organization.

Consider:

Scrutinize your determination. How have you reacted to failure? How strong is your FQ? Can you put failures behind you and stay determined to reach your goals?

EFFORT

**Consistency of effort is the
hallmark of a great leader.**

I used to think that effort was the key to being a great athlete, great student, or great leader. But what I found in my coaching and teaching was that too many athletes and students could give you a great effort on Monday, Tuesday, and Wednesday, but for some reason they couldn't find that same effort on Thursday, Friday, and Saturday. I, therefore, came to the conclusion that the difference between a good athlete, student, or leader and a great athlete, student, or leader was not effort but **CONSISTENCY OF EFFORT.** The great ones are the same every day. Once the great players crossed those lines for practice, once the great students entered the classroom, and once the great leaders arrived at their office, they could dig down and daily find that consistent effort.

Throughout the book, I've often recognized three leaders for whom I have great regard: Gordie Gillespie, Father/Bishop Roger Kaffer and Dr. Jack Orr. If I had to pick only one characteristic of the ATTITUDE acronym that I respect them for, the one trait that each of them exhibited to the highest degree, it would be the E. They didn't give effort; they truly gave consistency of effort. If I were to pick the three leaders with whom I worked who put in the most hours and who genuinely cared about the institutions and the people within the institutions they represented, those three would again be Gordie, the bishop, and Jack. How fortunate I have been to work with these three leaders!

I don't even know where to begin to address the consistency of effort that Gordie lived. He developed outstanding athletic programs at two colleges — Lewis College and the College of St. Francis —while *simultaneously* coaching high school football. At both private colleges, his athletic programs accomplished three of the most important things that small, private schools need: enrollment, profit, and publicity.

After building the athletic program at Lewis, Gordie asked me to go with him to St. Francis. As mentioned earlier, he took St. Francis athletics from forty-five student-athletes in three sports to 377 in fourteen sports. And he did this at a college that played no sports on-campus. For the first eleven years of the program, every sport played in or on off-campus facilities. Because every scholarship given in the formation of these programs was only partial (no full-rides), this addition of students gen-erated substantial profit for the institution. Not only did he bring student-athletes to both Lewis and St. Francis, but he also brought winning programs. The publicity generated by these programs, includ-ing three NAIA baseball national championships at Lewis and one at St Francis, helped in their respec-tive development and admissions offices.

Gordie also did what many athletic directors fail to do: he cared about the student-athletes in all sports, both male and female. He made an effort every day to let every person know how important he or she was. He taught all his coaches by his example. He would finish football practice at six and not go home for dinner. Instead, he would go in his football practice gear to the women's volleyball matches. This was for *every* home game. He also administered every home men's basketball games and attended all the home women's basketball games—a team he coached one year. He supported every sport to show every athlete, not just the athletes in the so-called "major" sports, how much he cared. There was no such thing as major and minor sports in his leadership.

There may not be a coach in America who has coached as many athletes as Gordie. He coached basketball for seventeen years, football for forty, and baseball for fifty-nine. The number of athletes he has coached is somewhere between 2,500 and 3,000. It's also amazing how much he is respected by those who played for him. So many of us, including me, see him as one of the most incredible people we have ever met. That was the impact of his leadership. Somehow, he was able to touch individually the thousands of athletes who played for him. Coaches who coach one sport often don't have the impact Gordie has had on athletes in three sports. He is the most respected and admired coach I've ever met.

When you have a leader like Gordie, you have no choice but to give your best effort as you observe his example. You also see daily what servant leadership is all about.

Father, then Bishop, Roger Kaffer was Gordie's equal in leadership and consistency of effort. He was first a priest. He was always available to help those in need. I was with him one night at midnight when he took a call from an inmate in prison to whom he was ministering. Whenever the students at Providence lost a parent, he was at the funeral service. When those who knew him ran into difficult times, he was the first person they called. He once told me, "People are more important than things," and he lived that maxim. He dropped the "thing" he was doing whenever those in need called.

The time he put into his work bordered on unbelievable. When he came to us at Providence as our principal, we were in deep financial trouble. To keep doing his priestly duties, which always came first, and to lead Providence in the midst of its fiscal problems, he had to work two full-time jobs. I can often remember sitting with his secretary, Margaret Videtich, who knew his workload better than anyone, and talking about his work ethic. Father worked with a dictaphone, and Margaret would often tell me that after dictating all his correspondence, it was not uncommon for him to say, "It's 2 a. m., and I better call it a day." Whenever he stopped his dictating, there was one thing for certain. He always said seven o'clock Mass at school to start the day. His energy was incomprehensible.

He took his principal duties so seriously, he did something I've never heard of any principal anywhere ever doing. Every year he visited the homes of all the freshmen and transfer students at Providence. After four years, he had visited the home of every student in the school. Was there ever a principal who has been in the homes of all his students? I highly doubt it. That was the dedication Bishop Kaffer gave in all his working years.

When you worked at Providence High School, you would not even think of complaining about the hours you worked, because they were minimal compared to your leader's. Bishop Kaffer's consistency of effort never ceased to amaze me.

Jack Orr was a leader like Gordie and Bishop Kaffer. When he became president of the College of St. Francis, it also was in deep financial trouble. In addition to fiscal problems, he was at a very small college; our full-time enrollment was under five hundred students. A high school basketball player we were recruiting told me he really liked our college, but he said, "Coach, your entire college is smaller than my high school senior class." Needless to say, we lost that recruit. That was the perception and the reality that Jack was up against when he became president.

Jack began his work at St. Francis with the faculty. He set high standards when hiring new faculty. They had to be committed to their discipline and to the students. He wanted to be sure that the students who chose to attend St. Francis would be the recipients of a high-quality education. His faculty standards enabled St. Francis to become the highly respected academic institution it is today.

I will never forget Jack's instructions to Gordie and me when we came aboard. He said he wanted three things from us. First, we were to expand the athletic program so we could attract more enrollees to the college. Second, we were to establish a comprehensive intramural program so we could offer "an activity for every student." Third, Jack held us to the same high standards he held faculty. He said he wanted an athletic program that would be run with complete integrity. His final statement was, "Give us a program of integrity, and winning will be a bonus." Pressure to win never came from Jack during our nineteen years with him; but pressure to do things the right way never wavered. In the last analysis, we did both.

Jack's work, like Gordie's and the bishop's, knew no hours. He was totally dedicated to the advancement of St. Francis, financially and educationally. His dedication led him to increase enrollment, as previously mentioned, from 436 students upon his arrival to 4,200 students, including 3,400 part-time on campus and in nineteen states. He was the leader of that initiative, and it demanded a great deal of time and travel.

In addition to the above, Jack was concerned with the welfare of everyone on campus. He didn't just know his fellow administrators, faculty, and coaches. He knew almost everyone on campus.

When you walked the campus with Jack, he not only acknowledged everyone, he knew the great majority of them by name. He knew the secretaries, the maintenance men and women, and the cleaning ladies. He knew them—and he cared about them. One particular year, we were having a very difficult time financially and really had to fine-tune our budget. He took the average salary of the college personnel and gave that figure a 4 percent raise. That dollar amount was the raise everyone got across the board, thereby giving the least paid people the highest percentage increase. He appreciated the work of everyone, but he knew that those being paid the least were also raising families. That was a tough decision—one not favored by many who received minimal raises percentage-wise—but it showed the commitment Jack had to those whose work often went unseen and unappreciated.

Jack was a superb leader, and when you worked with him, you tried your best to emulate his dedication and work ethic.

The leadership of Gordie, Bishop Kaffer, and Jack are examples of how consistency of effort can lead to successful execution. Gordie built two highly successful collegiate athletic programs; Bishop Kaffer saved Providence High School; and Jack laid the foundation for the national prominence St. Francis enjoys today. For their efforts, all three of them received many honors and, like all revered leaders, they accepted their accolades with humility. As John

Wooden used to say, "Give all the credit away." They did just that, and they stayed true to the following quote from Coach Wooden:

> **Talent is God-given, so be humble.**
> **Fame is man-given, so be grateful.**
> **But conceit is self-given, and you better be careful.**

A leader's effort is his or her calling card. I believe a leader's consistency of effort is the primary concept that earns him or her respect. If the leader is not committed to effort, why would those who work for him or her give their all? The leader sets the example, and his or her dedicated effort makes all the difference in the overall work ethic of the organization.

Consider:

Analyze your effort. Is your effort consistent? Do you think the people in your organization have *caught* your effort?

EPILOGUE

I hope you have enjoyed reading this book on how attitude affects leadership. I also hope you will think about the characteristics of a good attitude and how a good attitude makes for a quality leader. Finally, I hope you found some concepts in the book that you have not considered before in your leadership philosophy. After reflecting on these concepts, I hope they enhance your leadership role.

ATTITUDE

One person's attitude does make a difference and your philosophy of criticism is important to your communication skills.

TEAMWORK

Strong leaders build strong teams and give credit to their teams.

TOUGHNESS

Toughness enables you to handle critics and to demand excellence from your people. Leaders can also give the gift of toughness to their constituents.

INTELLIGENCE

Developing listening skills and persevering in core values make for an intelligent leader.

THANK YOU

Thanking and complimenting **ALL** your people goes a long way.

YOU

Your work ethic leads to your success; great leaders surround themselves with great people; and quality leaders do all they can to help others.

DETERMINATION

Nothing great is accomplished without great determination and a strong FQ (failure quotient).

EFFORT

Consistency of effort is the hallmark of a great leader.

SPEAKING ENGAGEMENTS

The characteristics of a successful leader are underscored by attitude. In his speaking engagements, Pat Sullivan provides the simple, practical concepts and attitude adjustments that lead to true leadership success and that will allow business leaders and their teams to meet their goals.

As a sought-after public speaker, Pat has helped numerous corporations improve their teamwork and employee effectiveness through his real-life experiences and observations. Pat is based in the Chicago area but speaks throughout the U.S. and globally.

If you would like Pat to speak to your organization, he can be reached by email at

psully100@comcast.net.

You may also connect with him through his website at either of these domains: www.coachpatsullivan.com or www.leadersattitude.com.

Made in the USA
Middletown, DE
28 May 2015